First World War
and Army of Occupation
War Diary
France, Belgium and Germany

58 DIVISION
Divisional Troops
291 Brigade Royal Field Artillery
22 January 1917 - 31 May 1919

WO95/2995/5

The Naval & Military Press Ltd
www.nmarchive.com
Published in association with The National Archives

Published by

The Naval & Military Press Ltd

Unit 10 Ridgewood Industrial Park,

Uckfield, East Sussex,

TN22 5QE England

Tel: +44 (0) 1825 749494

www.naval-military-press.com

www.nmarchive.com

This diary has been reprinted in facsimile from the original. Any imperfections are inevitably reproduced and the quality may fall short of modern type and cartographic standards.

© Crown Copyright
Images reproduced by permission of The National Archives, London, England, 2015.

Contents

Document type	Place/Title	Date From	Date To
Heading	WO95/2995-4		
Heading	B E F 28 Division Troops 291 Brigade R.F.A. (Formerly 2/2 London Bde To May 1916) 1917 Jan 1919 May		
Heading	War Diary 291st Bde R.F.A. Vol 192		
War Diary	Heytesbury	22/01/1917	22/01/1917
War Diary	Southampton	22/01/1917	22/01/1917
War Diary	Havre	23/01/1917	24/01/1917
War Diary	Abbeville	25/01/1917	25/01/1917
War Diary	Wavans	26/01/1917	26/01/1917
War Diary	Lucheux	06/02/1917	18/02/1917
War Diary	Bailleumont	24/02/1917	22/03/1917
Operation(al) Order(s)	Operation Orders No. 5 By Lieut-Colonel W.T. Odam Commanding 291st Bde. RFA. Appendix A	19/03/1917	19/03/1917
War Diary	Adinfer	22/03/1917	22/03/1917
War Diary	Moyenville	25/03/1917	30/03/1917
War Diary	Battle H Q T 25 A77 51 BSW	01/04/1917	02/04/1917
War Diary	Moyenville	03/04/1917	05/04/1917
War Diary	Battn H Q	06/04/1917	13/04/1917
War Diary	Ervillers	14/04/1917	14/04/1917
War Diary	Battle H Q As B 17 B 36 Map 57c NW	15/04/1917	23/04/1917
Miscellaneous			
Heading	War Diary Of 291st Bde R.F.A. From 3/5/17 To 21/5/17		
War Diary	Battle H Q As B 17b 3.6 May 57c NW	03/05/1917	21/05/1917
Heading	War Diary Of 291 Bde R.F.A. From 29/5/17 To 30/6/17		
War Diary	Battle H Q B 17 B 3.6	29/05/1917	30/06/1917
War Diary	Ervillers	04/07/1917	04/07/1917
War Diary	Fricourt	11/07/1917	11/07/1917
War Diary	Ytres	17/07/1917	18/07/1917
War Diary	Metz en Couture	29/07/1917	29/07/1917
War Diary	Havrincourt	02/08/1917	02/08/1917
War Diary	Boyelle	05/08/1917	07/08/1917
War Diary	St Leger	08/08/1917	20/08/1917
War Diary	Ervillers	21/08/1917	26/08/1917
War Diary	Hopoutre	27/08/1917	27/08/1917
War Diary	Dickebusche	30/08/1917	31/08/1917
War Diary	Nr Dickebranch	02/09/1917	03/09/1917
War Diary	Nr Herzeele	06/09/1917	07/09/1917
War Diary	Vlamatinge	14/09/1917	14/09/1917
War Diary	La Belle Alliance	20/09/1917	30/09/1917
War Diary	In The Field	04/10/1917	29/10/1917
War Diary	BHQ Vlamertinghe	31/10/1917	02/11/1917
War Diary	Wormhoudt Nieurlet	03/11/1917	12/11/1917
War Diary	BHQ. Attin	04/12/1917	04/12/1917
War Diary	Elverdinghe	09/12/1917	09/12/1917
War Diary	Adelphi House	10/12/1917	31/12/1917
War Diary	B.H.Q.	12/01/1918	12/01/1918
War Diary	Adelphi House	13/01/1918	13/01/1918

War Diary	Elverdinghe		22/01/1918	23/01/1918
War Diary	Domart		28/01/1918	28/01/1918
War Diary	Carrepuis		29/01/1918	29/01/1918
War Diary	Bretigny		30/01/1918	30/01/1918
War Diary	Vilette		31/01/1918	31/01/1918
War Diary	B.H.Q. Vilette		01/02/1918	03/02/1918
War Diary	Sinceny		15/02/1918	28/02/1918
War Diary	Elverdinghe		18/01/1918	18/01/1918
War Diary	B.H.Q. Sinceny		01/03/1918	21/03/1918
War Diary	Pierremande		31/03/1918	31/03/1918
Heading	Headquarters, 291st Brigade R.F.A. April 1918			
War Diary	B.H.Q. Pierremande		01/04/1918	05/04/1918
War Diary	Boutillerie		06/04/1918	06/04/1918
War Diary	Fouelloy		07/04/1918	30/04/1918
War Diary	B.H.Q. Beugny L'abbe		03/05/1918	03/05/1918
War Diary	Pont Remy		16/05/1918	16/05/1918
War Diary	Bourdon		17/05/1918	17/05/1918
War Diary	V.15.a.63 57d		18/05/1918	31/05/1918
War Diary	B.H.Q. Sheet 57d V. 15 A 63		01/06/1918	07/06/1918
War Diary	Contay		09/06/1918	09/06/1918
War Diary	St Laurence		11/06/1918	19/06/1918
War Diary	Bavelincourt		20/06/1918	20/06/1918
War Diary	D 7 A 8.7 Sheet 62 D		21/06/1918	30/06/1918
War Diary	D 7a 87 Sheet 62 D		01/07/1918	29/07/1918
Heading	291st Brigade. R.F.A. August. 1918			
War Diary	B.H.Q. Map Rife Senlis Hats 62d NE 62c NW 1/2000. Bazieux		02/08/1918	02/08/1918
War Diary	Vaux-Sur-Somme		08/08/1918	08/08/1918
War Diary	Jailly Laurette		09/08/1918	09/08/1918
War Diary	Balard Wood		10/08/1918	12/08/1918
War Diary	Chineleon Valley		19/08/1918	25/08/1918
War Diary	Maricourt		26/08/1918	26/08/1918
War Diary	Valley		27/08/1918	27/08/1918
War Diary	Blarlly De Comend		28/08/1918	30/08/1918
War Diary	Lear Well 110		31/08/1918	31/08/1918
War Diary	B.H.Q. Ref Sheet 62c Nr Hem		05/09/1918	06/09/1918
War Diary	Aizecourt Le-Bas		07/09/1918	17/09/1918
War Diary	Quarry E.18.c		18/09/1918	24/09/1918
War Diary	Nr Ronssoy		25/09/1918	29/09/1918
War Diary	BHQ. Nr. Bellicourt Le Catelet		01/10/1918	09/10/1918
War Diary	Aizecourt-Le-Bas		11/10/1918	12/10/1918
War Diary	Maroc		18/10/1918	18/10/1918
War Diary	Dourges		19/10/1918	19/10/1918
War Diary	Auchy		20/10/1918	20/10/1918
War Diary	Aix		21/10/1918	08/11/1918
War Diary	Wiers		09/11/1918	09/11/1918
War Diary	Ecacheries		11/11/1918	21/11/1918
War Diary	Wiers		29/11/1918	29/11/1918
War Diary	Beloeil		01/12/1918	01/12/1918
War Diary	Belgium		13/12/1918	30/12/1918
War Diary	B.H.Q. Beloeil		01/04/1919	01/04/1919
War Diary	Belgium		30/04/1919	30/04/1919
War Diary	B.H.Q. Beloeil Belgium		01/05/1919	31/05/1919

WO 95/2995/4

BEF

58. DIVISION TROOPS

291 BRIGADE R.F.A.
(FORMERLY 2/2 LONDON BDE TO MAY 1916)

1917 JAN — 1919 MAY

Box 2995

Vol 72

WAR DIARY

2.91st Bde R.F.A

WAR DIARY

or

INTELLIGENCE SUMMARY.
(Erase heading not required.)

Army Form C. 2118.

262nd Brigade R.F.A.

Instructions regarding War Diaries and Intelligence Summaries are contained in F. S. Regs., Part II. and the Staff Manual respectively. Title pages will be prepared in manuscript.

Place	Date	Hour	Summary of Events and Information	Remarks and references to Appendices
HEYTESBURY	22/1/17	2.30 pm	Left for Southampton	WD/H
SOUTHAMPTON	22/1/17	7 pm	Completed Embarkation and sailed in S/S Archimedes for HAVRE	WD/H
HAVRE	23/1/17	7.30 am	Arrived at HAVRE and disembarked. Men marched to No 2 Rest Camp	WD/H
– " –	24/1/17	9 pm	Entrained and left ABBEVILLE due here 7am 25/1/17	WD/H
ABBEVILLE	25/1/17	6.35 pm	Arrived ABBEVILLE 10½ hours late & received instructions to proceed to AUXI le CHATEAU	WD/H
WAYANS	26/1/17	–	Arrived AUXI le CHATEAU at 11.50 pm 25/1/17, detrained and received orders to march to WAYANS and billet	WD/H
LUCHEUX	6/2/17	–	Marched for LUCHEUX at 8.45 am arriving 2 pm. En route received instructions re: reorganization of Divisional Artillery, by which D/291 Battery received a section of 4.5 Hows and Captain Fawcus from D/293 Battery which was broken up. Captain Fawcus reported with his section	WD/H
LUCHEUX	7/2/17		Transfer of section as above completed	WD/H
– " –	10/2/17		Major T J Gatehouse +52 Rank & File joined from each Battery by 9am	WD/H

T2134. Wt. W708—776. 500000. 4/15. Sir J. C. & S.

2

WAR DIARY of 31st Brigade RHA

Army Form C. 2118.

WAR DIARY or INTELLIGENCE SUMMARY.
(Erase heading not required.)

Place	Date	Hour	Summary of Events and Information	Remarks and references to Appendices
			at BEAUMETZ.	
LUCHEUX	10/2/17	—	A A "D" Batteries being attached to 48th Brigade RHA while C Battery is attached to 246th Brigade RHA at BAILLEUMONT.	M.S.W.
LUCHEUX	13/2/17	—	While the Brigade was at NAVANS 4 horses (seven) died from J which died of contagious pleuro-pnemonia caught either on the boat or train. The other three were sent on being cases brought about by the extremes of temperature from boat to No 2 Rest camp at Havre when the night temperature was down to 17° FAH, and then from train to picquet lines in the open at Chelers, the regt. at NAVANS there a temperature of 9° Far. No further cases have occurred to date.	M.S.W.
LUCHEUX	18/2/17	—	Personnel of A, B, "D" Batteries transferred from 48th Brigade RHA to 246th Brigade RHA and were attached to A, C, "D" Batteries respectively there being the Batteries which they were to relieve.	M.S.W.
BAILLEUMONT	24/2/17		A, B, C, Batteries went in one section of personnel to take over from A, C, "D" Batteries respectively of 246th Brigade RHA. [ ] "D" Battery went in one section

WAR DIARY of 1291st Brigade R.F.A.

complete with {Horses {Guns} "D" 246th Brig: rewiring two 9"heir guns (Hand Phos)

[signature] Lt Col
Commdg 291st Brigade R.F.A.

WAR DIARY of 291st Brigade R.H.A.

Army Form C. 2118.

WAR DIARY or INTELLIGENCE SUMMARY.
(Erase heading not required.)

Instructions regarding War Diaries and Intelligence Summaries are contained in F.S. Regs., Part II. and the Staff Manual respectively. Title pages will be prepared in manuscript.

Place	Date	Hour	Summary of Events and Information	Remarks and references to Appendices
BAILLEULMONT	25/8/17		A,B,C Batteries took over guns complete from the Batteries of 246th Brigade "A" from "A", "B" from "C" & abutting from "B". Batteries respectively. "D" Battery completed their relief, putting their own guns in.	
"	26/8/17		The 291st Brigade H.Q.rs relieved the 246th Brigade H.Q.rs at 10.30 a.m. the relief of Batteries having been reported complete by that time and all 246th Brigade personnel clear.	
"	6/3/17		Small raid by Coocke and our trenches at the foot of LIMERICK LANE in C 2.4.d	
"	25/8/17		in depth. Having retired from our front "B" Battery 291st Brigade was closed to give front "support" infantry from #T 14 central to "B" Battery BOIRY BECQUEREKE (Reference map 51B SW 20000) The Battery being placed in opposite under Lt.Col.H.N. Clark Comdg 290th Aug RGA	
"	27/8/17		H Qrs with B.C. "D" Battery moved to ADINFER WOOD (THE LODGE)	

Moore
Lt Col
Comdg 291st Brigade R.H.A.

Appendix A

SECRET.   COPY No. 11

OPERATION ORDERS   No. 5.
BY
LIEUT-COLONEL W.T. ODAM
COMMANDING, 291st., BDE., RFA.

----

1. The NORTHERN BOUNDARY of 58th DIVISION is BOIRY BECQUERELLE - BOISLEUX AU MONT - FISHEUX all inclusive.
The SOUTHERN BOUNDARY of 58th DIVISION ADINFER - ST LEGER - CROISELLE all exclusive.

The 173rd Infantry Brigade will hold line from BOIRY BACQUERELLE inclusive along road through T.14.b. to ST. LEGER MILL at T.21.d.9.1

The 30th DIVISION has relieved the 175th Infantry Brigade north of BOIRY BACQUERELLE.

2. A/291st., Brigade, R.F.A. will relieve C/150th Brigade, and will support the left of 173rd Infantry Brigade from S 14 CENTRAL to BOIRY BACQUERELLE.

3. A/291st., Bde., R.F.A. will march at 8.30 a.m. on the morning of 20th March. The Battery Commander will go forward at once and reconnoitre for a position to cover frontage as in para 2 of these orders. The Battery Commander will get in touch with the Infantry Battalion Commander, and establish a close Liason with him.

4. Suggested position for Wagon Lines HENDECOURT or ADINFER.

5. Great care must be exercised in occupation of position, if really necessary, this will not be carried out until after dusk, but with careful leading the occupation may be able to be carried out in day light.

6. Brigade Headquarters will remain at BAILLEULMONT, where reports will be sent.

7. Please acknowledge.

                                                W. Odam
                                        LIEUT - COLONEL,
                                COMMANDING, 291st., BRIGADE, R.F.A.

Bde., Hdqrs.,
19.3.17.
Issued at 10.30 pm.

No. 1 copy to C.R.A. by Orderly.
 " 2 "   " 173rd Infantry Bde.,   by Orderly.
 " 3 "   " 174th Infantry Bde.,   "   "
 " 4 "   " 175th Infantry Bde.,   "   "
 " 5 "   " "A" Battery - 291st.Bde.,"   "
 " 6 "   " "B"   "   -   "   "   "   "
 " 7 "   " "C"   "   -   "   "   "   "
 " 8 "   " "D"   "   -   "   "   "   "
 " 9 - 12 FILED.

Army Form C. 2118.

WAR DIARY
or
INTELLIGENCE SUMMARY.
(Erase heading not required.)

29th August 1918
Vol 4

Place	Date	Hour	Summary of Events and Information	Remarks and references to Appendices
ADINFER	27/3		Head Quarters and B,C,D. Batteries moved from BAILLEULMONT to ADINFER. H.Q. in the wood and the Batteries in vicinity of ADINFER.	
MOYENVILLE	28/3		Brig H.Q moved in evening of this day. B Battery occupied a position in outskirts of HAMELINCOURT. "D" Battery behind a railway embankment close to MOYENVILLE. C Battery remained at ADINFER which was the Brigade rendezvous.	
—"—	29/3		58th Divisional Artillery attacked to 21st Divisional Artillery for instruction pending the 291st Brigade forming a Sub-Group under Lt.Col Fitzgerald commanding 95th Brigade RFA.	B
—"—			B + C Batteries moved up unengaged positions in vicinity of ST LEGER in O.O. No 33	
—	30/3		to support attack on CROISILLES	
—	—		H.Q.s moved to Battle H.Q. for the attack. (Both H.A. 7.25 a 77 Map 51BSW)	
BATTLE H.Q 7.25 a 77 on 51ASW	Apl 2	5.15am	Barrage opened and by 7.30 attack was reported as successful orders for advance issued also "draw of the day" 5 Maps and Company commanding the 21st Division returned	
MOYENVILLE	Apl 3rd		C + D Batteries moved to new positions near ST LEGER and preparations commenced for operations on a larger scale.	

WAR DIARY
or
INTELLIGENCE SUMMARY.

Army Form C. 2118

29th Brigade RFA

Place	Date	Hour	Summary of Events and Information	Remarks and references to Appendices
MOYENVILLE	Apr 5		Continued to HINDENBURG LINE commenced at 7am from A Batth Hd. Quarters at T.25.a.77 May 5.8.5am	
	Apr 6		Batteries continued bombardment	
	Apr 7		Batteries continued bombardment	
BEHAGNIES	Apr 8		Bombardment continued	
"	Apr 9		do	
"	Apr 10		do	
"	Apr 11		Z day. All batteries fired a barrage. The attack successful at first, at the end enemy infantry was held in front further	
"	Apr 12		2 batteries bombardment of Riencourt trail	
"	Apr 13		Attack by Infantry Brigade. Attack unsuccessful	
"	Apr 14		Bombardment of enemy trench wiring point. Attack by 110th Infantry Brigade bombing Eastward. Artillery retaliated a black some sort of trench party were relieved by 12th Brigade RFA 10th British Machine completed.	
"	Apr 15		SS fixed. Reconnections other made by CMT commanding 2nd Battn also CRA and 29th RA Battery arrived at Hamelincourt positions to commence for new position to attack on BULLEN COURT	
ERVILLERS	Apr 16		The 58th Division	

WAR DIARY or INTELLIGENCE SUMMARY

Army Form C. 2118.

War Diary 291st Brigade R.F.A.

Place	Date	Hour	Summary of Events and Information	Remarks and references to Appendices
Battle H.Q. B.17.b.36 Map 57c NW	15/4/17		Artillery being formed into Bde Groups being called the 58th Divisional Group. under Lt. Col. A. Clark. Battle H.Quarters established at B.17.b.3.6. Close to Croix Haut Quentin. All Batteries occupies previous section of ECOUST ST MEIN the same enemy shelled the ECOUST valley very freely early this morning causing casualties & damage to material. Capt. Vause & Lt. Johnston severely wounded and 2/Lt. A. Forth & 2/Lt. H.T. Coreland killed also 3 gunners killed and 5 wounded all belonging to "C" Battery. 2/Lt. H.T. Miles of "D" Battery was also wounded + 1 gunner killed & two wounded Capt. J.R. Faure + 2/Lt. H.S. Miles also 1 recruits "C" Battery had 2 men killed	(D) (D) (D) (D)
	16/4/17		and two wounded from enemy bombardment on this day. "C" Battery had it new recruits from Grenades also for "C" Battery	(D)
	17/4/17		positions are changed. Capt. Archie received command temporarily of "C" Battery. Capt. E.C. Young posted to command "C" Battery (through Division)	(D)
	20/4/17 23/4/17		The effect of the terribly bad weather and extremely hard work & dirt in bringing up munitions too his reinless in 115 deaths & 321 evacuations to hospital Veterinary sections. The horses have stood the atmospheric of the and front	

Army Form C. 2118.

WAR DIARY
or
INTELLIGENCE SUMMARY.
(Erase heading not required.)

Place	Date	Hour	Summary of Events and Information	Remarks and references to Appendices
			has been 12th pack infantry the 9th whole broken there return from early July to March 23rd.	

MStein
Col
Comdg Sqn Brigade R.S.A.

Vol 5

CONFIDENTIAL
****

WAR DIARY

OF

201st Bde R.F.A.

From 3/5/17
To 21/5/17

WAR DIARY or INTELLIGENCE SUMMARY

Army Form C. 2118

291st Brigade RFA

Place	Date	Hour	Summary of Events and Information	Remarks and references to Appendices
Battle Hd at B.17.b.3.6 map 57cNW	3/5/17	am	Supported the attack by (62nd Division) 185th Brigade on BULLECOURT which was unsuccessful although the first objective was taken but lost again within ten hours.	(1)
		3.30	Attacks continued but without success.	(2)
	4/5/17			(3)
	7/5/17	3.45	Supported the attack of 20th Brigade (7th Division) in BULLECOURT in which was a partial success, getting into village from EAST end.	(4)
	8/5/17	11am	Attack renewed & made further small gains.	(5)
	9/5/17	12 noon	A third attack made, but in the enemy the Brigade (7/) were back in same position as on 7th inst.	(6)
	10/5/17	7am	A further attack made on BULLECOURT & an advance so far from it held.	(7)
	11/5/17	-	Supported attack of 91st Brigade who relieved 20th but no further progress made.	(8)
	14/5/17 15/5/17		Several more attacks made this day without success. 174th Infy Brigade relieved 91st Brigade. This brought 58th Divn. Infantry into the line. Lt Cramsey killed whilst FOO.	(9)(10)(11)
	17/6/17	2am	2/5 Battalion of 174th Infy Brigade attacked successfully & BULLECOURT was at last in our hands. Enemy held trenches north of village	(12)

Army Form C. 2118

WAR DIARY
INTELLIGENCE SUMMARY

Place	Date	Hour	Summary of Events and Information	Remarks and references to Appendices
Ballydrain	18		Lt F Atkinson Killinan his way to Thoreton station a .... shot	
	3.6.17			
	21/5/17	3.45	2/6 Battn "A" Col 2nd (174th Inf Bgde) attacked BOIS TRENCH They attacked their objective but owing to heavy .... obstacles ... with machine guns the Battalion was driven back to original line Artillery good but .... barrage had been ..... without .... enough tip of 250 yds the infantry attack might have been more successful, as the ground in front .... have been thoroughly searched	

M Munro
Lt Col
Comdg 2/6 A&S.Hghdrs RHP

Vol 6

Confidential

War Diary
of 291 Bde RFA
from 29/5/17 to 31/4/17

WAR DIARY or INTELLIGENCE SUMMARY

Army Form C. 2118.

9th Bde RHA

Place	Date	Hour	Summary of Events and Information	Remarks and references to Appendices
Battle NR B1,2,3,6	22/4/17		The 29th Bde who had formed part of 60th Div Arty group were taken over by 58th Divisional Arty.	(M)
do	24/4/17		Reconnaissance for new positions for 2nd Bde Arty.	(M)
do	27/4/17 6am		The 29th Bde RHA who had formed part of 7th Divl Arty Group were taken over by 58th Divisional Arty.	(M)
do	24/4/17 10am		The 29th Bde RHA were taken over by 2nd Divl Arty.	(M)
do	28/4/17		The Relief of the Brigade by 38th IA Brigade commenced.	(M)
do	30/4/17 10am		The relief of the Brigade completed. The Brigade was withdrawn from action and went into rest.	(M)
			Casualties during the month of from 13 OR wounded 1 OR died of wounds.	

M^claw
Lt Col
Comdg 29th Bde RHA

WAR DIARY or INTELLIGENCE SUMMARY

Army Form C. 2118.

291st August R.A.A.

Place	Date	Hour	Summary of Events and Information	Remarks and references to Appendices
ERVILLERS	3/7/17	4.45 am	The Brigade marched to FRICOURT camping in MAMETZ BRIGADE CAMP	(222)
FRICOURT	4/5/17	6 am	The Brigade marched to YTRES camping on the southern exit of VALLULART WOOD	(ZZ)
YTRES	12/7/17		Section Trench Battery relieved sections of 291st Brigade covering the front of 173rd Infantry Brigade	(ZZ)
"	18/7/17		The relief of the 291st Brigade R.A.A. completed by 291st Brigade Battle Front Zenetin being south of METZ-en-COUTURE at Q.27.c.4.4. the Brigade forming the Right Group of 38th Divisional Front	(ZZ)
METZ en COUTURE	29/7/17	12.45 am	Raid carried out by a detachment from 2/4th Royal Fusiliers London Regt. The raid was successful but found no Bache in PLUSH TRENCH. In addition to fire from 291st Bdg R.A.A., 6-18pm 4-4.5 Hon. J 291st and 5-18/m of 181st August R.A.A. from placed on the disposal of O.C commanding Right Group	(WL)

M Nolan
Comdg
291st Brig R.A.A.

WAR DIARY or INTELLIGENCE SUMMARY

Form C. 2118.

291st Brigade R.F.A.

Instructions regarding War Diaries and Intelligence Summaries are contained in F.S. Regs., Part II. and the Staff Manual respectively. Title pages will be prepared in manuscript.

(Erase heading not required.)

Place	Date 1917	Hour	Summary of Events and Information	Remarks and references to Appendices
HARBINCOURT	2/8	10 am	The Brigade formed part of 9th Division 4th Corp 3rd Army	
–do–	3/8	10 am	" " " " " 40th Division 3rd Corp 3rd Army	
–do–	4/8	8 am	Half Brigade moved to take over from 51st Brigade R.F.A. at Boyelle	
Boyelle	5/8	8 am	2nd half of Brigade moved to Boyelle and relief completed at 12 noon. The Brigade coming under orders of 2nd Divl Artillery 7th Corp 3rd Army	
St Leger	6/8	10 pm	B.C./D. Batteries moved 1 gun each into new position to near ST LEGER VALLEY	
–	7/8	12 noon	The Brigade formed part of 2nd Divisional Artillery but in VI Corp 3rd Army	
ST LEGER	8/8	12 noon	Head Quarters tent to ST LEGER and B.C.D. Batteries moved the remainder of their guns into new positions	
ST LEGER	20/8	11.30 pm	Batteries moved into billets prior to moving bus at ERVILLERS	
ERVILLERS	25/8	3 am	Advance party sent to WINNEZEELE in Flanders	
–	26/8	8.30 pm	Head Quarters marched to ARRAS to entrain for the north.	
HONDPOUTRE	27/8	2.30 pm	Arrived at HONDPOUTRE and advance & complete in this place	
DICKEBUSCHE	30/8	7 pm	Brigade moved into new Wagon Lines in this area	
–	31/8	–	Half Batteries (personnel of) moved into the line new YPRES and took over from 10th Australian Divisional Artillery	

W Nham
Lt Col
Comdg 291st Brigade R.F.A.

WAR DIARY
or
INTELLIGENCE SUMMARY.
(Erase heading not required.)

Army Form C. 2118.

Place	Date	Hour	Summary of Events and Information	Remarks and references to Appendices
Dickebusch	2/9 3/9	7.30 am	Half Battery withdrew from position south of Ypres. Marched to billets WEST of HERZEELE. At horse rear transport from II Corps & XVIII Corps.	
HERZEELE	6/9	8.20	Brigade H.Qrs and one section per Battery marched to new map lines via VLAMATINGS. B.C. & section per Battery met a.b. return and took over HQ	
" HQ	7/9	8.20	Remainder of Batteries arrived and met with action. Issued — LEFT GROUP	
VLAMATINGS	14/9	12 noon	S/Lt Bn Artillery under Lt Col C Clifford. Brigade took over from 103rd Bry RFA HQrs at LA BELLE ALLIANCE.	
			S/Lt H. 7.0 AM Comdg 29th Bty took over command of Right Front Attack Group	
LA BELLE ALLIANCE	20/9	5.40 am	Supported the attack of 174th Brigade on the St JULIAN front. Attack completely successful. Received letter from Brig Gen Huggan O.C.B. congratulating 174 Brigade congratulating the Group on the same Gunnery	
	26/9 30/9	5.50 am 12 noon	Supported an attack by 175th Brigade which was successful. 2nd Lt O'Brien Killed. Lt Col Clifford assumed command of the Left Group	

Mackay
Capt
Comdy Sgt Anglehold RFA

WAR DIARY
or
INTELLIGENCE SUMMARY.

291st Brigade, R.F.A.

Place	Date	Hour	Summary of Events and Information	Remarks and references to Appendices
In the Field	4/10/17	—	Covered the Infantry of 48th Divn in action	(1)
do	10/10/17	—	Covered the Infantry of 48th Divn in action	(2)
do	16/10/17	—	Covered the Infantry of 48th Divn in action	(2)
do	26/10/17	—	Covered the Infantry of 63rd (RN) Divn in action	(2)
do	29/10/17	—	Covered the Infantry of 63rd (RN) Divn in action	(2)
			Casualties period in action 5/9/17 to 30/10/17 Officers — killed 2, wounded 1, gassed 8, sick 7 — Total 21 O.R. — killed 23, died of wounds 13, wounded 138, gassed 36, sick 75 — Total 285 Immediate awards for above period — Officers — DSO 1, MC 3 O.R. — DCM 3, MM 14	(1) (2) (2)

Lieut-Colonel, R.F.A. (T.)
Commanding 291st (London) Brigade R.F.A. (T.)

WAR DIARY
or
INTELLIGENCE SUMMARY.
(Erase heading not required.)

Place	Date	Hour	Summary of Events and Information	Remarks and references to Appendices
B.H.Q. Wormhoudt	Oct 31/1919	—	2 Sections of Batteries in action were relieved by Sections of 307 Bde. R.F.A.	
—do—	1/11/19	—	Relief complete	
—do—	2/11/19	—	Brigade marched to WORMHOUDT area	
Wormhoudt	3/11/19	—	Brigade marched to RECQUES area	
Munck	11/11/19	—		
Nieurlet	12/11/19	—	Brigade marched to ESTREHE area	
			Immediate awards for above period :—	
			Officers — M.C. 1	
			O.R. — D.C.M. —	

WAR DIARY
or
INTELLIGENCE SUMMARY.
(Erase heading not required.)

Army Form C. 2118

291st Brigade R.F.A.

Place	Date	Hour	Summary of Events and Information	Remarks and references to Appendices
BHQ Otken	Dec 14/9/17		Brigade proceeded by road via THIEMBRONNE, NIEURLET and WORMHOUDT to Wagon Lines EVERDINGHE arriving 8/12/17	
Rundenghe	Dec 9/12/17		Section of Batteries relieved sections of Batteries of 256th Brigade, R.F.A. in the line covering the Infantry of 58th Division	
Agatha House	Dec 10/12/17	9 am	Relief of 256th Brigade, R.F.A. by 291st Brigade, R.F.A. Completed. Lieut-Colonel T.F. Holland C.M.G., D.S.O., R.F.A. assumed temporary command of Brigade	
—	31/12/17	9 am	Lieut-Colonel M.S. Odam, R.F.A.(T) resumed command of Brigade	
			Casualties during period 1st to 31st December 1917	
			Officers — Nil	
			Other Ranks — Killed 6, wounded 6	

M.S. Odam
Lieut.-Colonel, R.F.A. (T.)
Commanding 291st (London) Brigade R.F.A. (T.)

WAR DIARY or INTELLIGENCE SUMMARY.   291st Brigade R.F.A.

Army Form C. 2118.

Place	Date	Hour	Summary of Events and Information	Remarks and references to Appendices
B1+0	1/11/18		Section of Battery relieved by 159th Army Brigade R.F.A	AR/20
Bayfhus Thorne	13/11/18		Relief complete	AR/20
Blanghy	27/23.11.18		Brigade proceeded by rail to MIERS BRETONNEUX for billets at DOMART-SOMME	AR/20
Domart	28/11/18		Brigade marched by road to CARREPUIS	AR/20
Carrepuis	29/11/18		Brigade marched by road to BRETIGNY	AR/20
Bretigny	30/11/18		Relief of French Artillery in the line commenced, 1st Day.	AR/20
"	3/11/18		Relief in progress	AR/20

D. Walker
Lieut. Colonel, R.F.A.
Commanding 291st (London) Brigade R.F.A. (T.F.)

WAR DIARY
or
INTELLIGENCE SUMMARY.

Army Form C. 2118.

291st Brigade RFA

Place	Date	Hour	Summary of Events and Information	Remarks and references to Appendices
R.H.Q Vill.	1/1/18		Relief of French Artillery in the line completed, covering Infty of 30th Divn.	
do	3/1/18		B.H.Q. moved to SINCENY. Wagon Lines moved from BRETIGNY to VILLETTE.	
Sincery	15/1/18		Covered the Infantry of 58th Divn in the line	
do	22/1/18		Covered the Infantry of 58th Divn in the line	
do	28/1/18		Covered the Infantry of 58th Divn in the line	
Blerancourt	18/1/18		Command of Brigade assumed by Lieut Col A.N.W. Dudley vice Lt Col N.W. Odam. Casualties during Feby 1918 – 1 Oth Ranks	

M. Odam Major.
Lieut-Colonel, R.F.A.
Commanding 291st (London) Brigade R.F.A. (T.F.)

Army Form C. 2118.

WAR DIARY
or
INTELLIGENCE SUMMARY.
(Erase heading not required.)

291st Brigade, R.F.A.

Place	Date	Hour	Summary of Events and Information	Remarks and references to Appendices
B.H.Q.	March 1918 1st		Covered the Infantry of 58th Division in the line	AD
do	19th		407th and 408th Batteries of 96th Army Brigade R.F.A attached to 291st Bde RFA	AD
do	21st		Enemy offensive commenced. B.H.Q. withdrawn to PIERREMANDE	AD
Pierremande	31st		Covered the Infantry of 58th Division in the line	AD
			Casualties during period 1st to 31st March 1918.	AD
			Officers (407 Bty) 1 wounded	AD
			Other Ranks 2 Killed 7 wounded (2-407 Bty)	AD

Lieut.-Colonel, R.F.A.
Commanding 291st (London) Brigade R.F.A. (T.)

58th Div.

WAR DIARY

Headquarters,

291st BRIGADE, R.F.A.

APRIL

1918

Army Form C. 2118.

WAR DIARY
INTELLIGENCE SUMMARY

of 291st Brigade, R.F.A.

(Erase heading not required.)

Instructions regarding War Diaries and Intelligence Summaries are contained in F.S. Regs., Part II. and the Staff Manual respectively. Title pages will be prepared in manuscript.

Place	Date	Hour	Summary of Events and Information	Remarks and references to Appendices
M/O Vignacourt	April 1918 1st		6 Batteries in action in Imerey Authieule area covering Toutencourt-Chavy	AP
			Bridges & Corders also Bodus front. Armoury Hony and Servon.	AP
do	2nd		Brigade relieved by French Artillery Regiment on the line.	AP
do	4/5		Brigade marched to Longeau and proceeded by train from there to Longeau	AP
Bondieres	6th		at Batteries in action night 6th/7th 4 guns each covering Villers Bretonneux front	AR
			to Nores Wood. Remaining sections to Rd Detail 58° Dec on 9th inst.	AR
Boudilly	7/23		Battery positions O.Ps Consolidated. Infantry Consolidated. Counter preparation	AR
			carried out at night. Bursts of fire and places of assembly, roads, tracks &c.	AP
	24th		Enemy attack opened at 5.15 am. Infantry refugee and Batteries withdrawn	AP
			to East Villers Bretonneux flanks. 8 pm 24th Batteries moved forward to	AP
			Support a successful attack launched at 10 pm same day.	AP
	25/29		Infantry consolidated and continues consolidation carried out	AP
	28/29		Brigade relieved in the line by 86th Army Brigade R.F.A.	AP
	29/30		a few	
	30		Brigade marched to ST PIERRE en route to LONG area to refit.	AP

A Dingley
Lieut.-Colonel, R.F.A.
Commanding 291st (London) Brigade R.F.A. (T.)

WAR DIARY
INTELLIGENCE SUMMARY
(Erase heading not required.)

Army Form C. 2118.

Place	Date	Hour	Summary of Events and Information	Remarks and references to Appendices
R.H.Q.	1918			
Burgin'l Abb.	May 3rd		Brigade marched by road to PONT REMY area	GD
Pont Remy	16th		Brigade marched by road to BOURDON	GD
Bourdon	17th		Brigade proceeded to CONTAY and sections relieved sections of 282nd Brigade R.F.A. in the line	GD
VISa. 6.3. S.P.	18th		Relief completed. Lt. Battery R.H.A. attached to 291st Brigade R.F.A. forming left Group. 58th Divisional Artillery, and covering Infantry of 58th Division in the line.	GD
-do-		16/30a	Bursts of fire on roads, back Communications Counter Preparations and Nightfiring Programmes carried out. Gun Positions of A's conducted add informed	GD GD
-do-	31st		Available 35th Division on left in operation for AVELUY WOOD Bombardment carried out by Group.	GD

A. Dunlop
Lieut.-Colonel, R.F.A.
Commanding 291st (London) Brigade R.F.A. (T.)

291st Brigade, R.F.A.

WAR DIARY
INTELLIGENCE SUMMARY
(Erase heading not required.)

Place	Date	Hour	Summary of Events and Information	Remarks and references to Appendices
H.Q.R. Bus les Artois B.3	June 1918 1st		Covering the Infantry of 18th Division who are being relieved by 18th Army Brigade R.F.A. in the Line.	AD
	7th		Brigade marched by road to ST SAUVEUR, forming part of 22nd Corps.	AD
Contay	9th		22nd Corps Artillery training.	AD
Beauvoir	11th		Lectures having and 1st June L Corps Area reconnoitered by B.C's	AD
do	19th		Brigade marched by road to BAZEINCOURT area.	AD
Bouzincourt	20th		Relieved 235th Brigade R.F.A. 47th Div in the Line forming Right Group 58th Div with 147th Bde R.F.A. 47th Army Bde R.F.A. attached	AD
D.7.a.6.7 Reference M.10	21st		Harassing fire carried out by day & night on roads, trenches, tracks and bridges, also M.G. emplacements. M.10 also awaited 18th Division left in bombardment of enemy trench system.	AD
	30			

Austin
Lieut.-Colonel, R.F.A.
Commanding 291st (London) Brigade R.F.A. (T)

WAR DIARY
INTELLIGENCE SUMMARY

Army Form C. 2118.

291 Brigade, R.F.A.

No. 7 1952

Place	Date	Hour	Summary of Events and Information	Remarks and references to Appendices
D/a 81 Sheet 62D	1918 July 12		Assisted 58th Australian Batn on right in raiding enemy trenches by 4 Batteries.	AS
	15th		A.C. Bty & 108th Army Brigade, RFA attacked Right Group	AS
	14th		C & D Btys 108 Army Brigade, RFA withdrawn to Wagon lines	AS
	21st		Co-operated in gas bombardment of enemy trenches and backs	AS
	23rd		Assisted in raid on enemy trenches, co-operating with Australian Group. 7 Batteries in action Zero 10 a.m.	AS
	28th		Two Chinese attacks put down according to raid by 5th Aust Division	AS
	29th		A & C/86 Bde RFA joined Group, Constituting Left Group with 290 Bde RFA as Sub-Group.	AS

J C Janvrin Capt
for Major, RFA
Comdg 291 Brigade, RFA

58th Divl. Artillery

291st BRIGADE, R. F. A.

AUGUST, 1918

WAR DIARY
or
INTELLIGENCE SUMMARY.
(Erase heading not required.)

Army Form C. 2118.

291st BRIGADE R.F.A.

Aug 5/17 — Aug 20

Place	Date	Hour	Summary of Events and Information	Remarks and references to Appendices
B.H.Q. Rob Roy Subs Special Station Sh 62D N.E. 62C N.W. Cayeux	Aug			
	2nd		Brigade relieved by 112th Brigade, 25th Division R.F.A. in the line. Wagon lines at Barencourt	RX
Cayeux	8th		Used in attack with Batteries as a Sub. Group near 58th S.A.	RX
	9th		Batteries advanced to positions near Sailly-Laurette	RX
Sailly-Laurette	10th		Attack continued under 4th Australian D.A. & Batteries advanced to positions	RX
Morlancourt Hood	11th/12th		Advance made by Armoured Wood, containing Chipilly Valley, formation of Division Force.	RX
Morlancourt Chipilly Valley	13th/25th		Capture of Bray, assisted by 3rd Australian D.A. Batteries advanced to positions East of Bray Chipilly	RX
Morlancourt Vallée	26th		Brigade moved forward to position North of Bray, under 58th Div.	RX
	27th		Attack continued. Batteries advanced to positions in Bariscourt Valley.	RX
Bariscourt Vallée	28th		Batteries advanced to Bois A Leck. A further advance was made	RX
	29th		and positions taken up near the Railway of Clery	RX
	31st		Batteries advanced to positions at junction of Wood Valley & Hill 110. And attack continued.	RX

21.00 110

V. Murphy Lt. Col R.F.A.
Commg 291 Brigade R.F.A.

WAR DIARY
or
INTELLIGENCE SUMMARY.

Army Form C.2118.

291 Brigade RFA Vol 21

Place	Date	Hour	Summary of Events and Information	Remarks and references to Appendices
Wittenbrock etc ARHEM	Sept 24th	1/5000	Batteries moved to HAUT ALLAINES attack continued	
		5ᵗʰ	Batteries moved to E. of AIZECOURT-LE-HAUT.	
		6ᵗʰ	Brigade withdrawn and moved N. of AIZECOURT-LE-HAUT under 58 Div. Arty only covering infantry of 58 Divn	
AIZECOURT-LE-BAS.	—	7ᵗʰ	Infantry 58 Divn attacked. Brigade withdrawn into reserve at AIZECOURT-LE-BAS	
		9ᵗʰ	In action near GURLU COURT, covering attack by 58 Divn on PEZIERES and EPEHY	
AIZECOURT-LE-BAS.	—	10ᵗʰ	Withdrawn into reserve at AIZECOURT-LE-BAS.	
QUARRY FIGC.	—	17ᵗʰ	Moved into action near VILLERS-FAUCON under 18ᵗʰ Divn. Arty	
	—	18ᵗʰ	Attack on EPEHY, PEZIERES and RONSSOY and LEMPIRE, Batteries advanced K.23 a.d.	
	—	19ᵗʰ	Attack continued by 53ʳᵈ Infantry Brigade, 18ᵗʰ Division	
	—	21ˢᵗ	Attack continued to ground S. of RONSSOY	
	—	24ᵗʰ	Enemy counter attack repulsed by concentrated Arty fire on TOMBOIS VALLEY F.3.d.	
N. RONSSOY	—	25ᵗʰ	Covering infantry of 27ᵗʰ American Divn under 4ᵗʰ Army Div Arty	
	—	27ᵗʰ	Heavy bombardment of hostile battery positions with "BB" Shell.	
	—	29ᵗʰ	Commenced attack on HINDENBURG LINE at LE CATELET and GOUY by 27ᵗʰ Amer. Divn	

Lieut.-Colonel, R.F.A.
Commanding 291st (Lonsboro) Brigade R.F.A. (T.F.)

WAR DIARY / INTELLIGENCE SUMMARY

Army Form C. 2118.

58Dy
291 Brigade, RFA.

Place	Date	Hour	Summary of Events and Information	Remarks and references to Appendices
MAR Q	1918			
BELLICOURT	Oct 1st	1?	Attack on LE CATELET proceeded - Batteries covering Infantry of 29th Ama Div.	
LE CATELET	4th	4?	Batteries advanced to position in GOUY covering Infantry of 38th Div.	
-do-		8?	Attack on VILLERS-OUTREAUX commenced by 38th Div.	
-do-		9?	Brigade withdrew to Wagon lines in LONGAVESNES area	
ATTECOURT LE BAS		11?	Entrained at PERONNE	
		12?	Detrained at BULLY-GRENAY to billets at MAROC	
MAROC		18th	Brigade marched to DOURGES en route to line	
DOURGES		19th	Relieved 148th Army Bde RFA. C/291 Battery in action near ORCHIES	
AUCHY		20?	Brigade advanced from near ORCHIES to AIX. C/291 advanced section to Remainder of Brigade in main guard - Covering 175th Infy Bde. 58 Div.	
AIX		21	Advance continued to RONGY	
-do-		23rd	Registration Ranging and ???? cutting vicinity of FORTE DE MAULDE.	
-do-		26?	Q/B D Batteries advanced to RUE DOMBRE, after Enemy in advancing F'F DE MAULDE	
-do-		27?	Relieved by 290th Brigade, R.F.A. Withdrew to AIX in Divisional Reserve	
-do-		31	In Divisional reserve	

Lieut.-Colonel, R.F.A.
Commanding 291st (London) Brigade R.F.A. (T.)

WAR DIARY
INTELLIGENCE SUMMARY

291 Brigade, R.F.A.

Army Form C. 2118.

Place	Date	Hour	Summary of Events and Information	Remarks and references to Appendices
	1918			
Aix	Nov 1st		In Divisional Reserve	
		8"	Brigade marched to VIERS - (sections of "B" and "D" Batteries covering advance of 175th Infantry Brigade	
		9"	Advance continued to ECACHERIES. Sections of "B" and "D" Btys in action	
VIERS		11"	Hostilities ceased at 1100 hours.	
ECACHERIES		21"	Brigade marched to billets in VIERS area	
VIERS		29"	Brigade marched to billets in BEAULIN area.	

Murphy Lieut Colonel, R.F.A.,
Comdg. 291 Brigade, R.F.A.

Army Form C. 2118.

WAR DIARY
INTELLIGENCE SUMMARY.
(Erase heading not required.)

29 Brigade RFA

Place	Date	Hour	Summary of Events and Information	Remarks and references to Appendices
	1918			
BELOEIL BELGIUM	Dec 1st to Dec 30th		Periodical & Educational training carried out. Coalmines, Crystals and Demolitions viewed for demobilization.	NY

H Knyvett Wolff Lt Col

WAR DIARY or **INTELLIGENCE SUMMARY**

Army Form C. 2118.

291ST LONDON BRIGADE, R.F.A.

Place	Date	Hour	Summary of Events and Information	Remarks and references to Appendices
B.H.Q. BELOEIL, BELGIUM.	April 1919 1st to 30th		Nil.	

[signature]
for Major, R.F.A.
Commanding 291. Brigade, R.F.A.

WAR DIARY

INTELLIGENCE SUMMARY. 55th RFA

(Erase heading not required.)

Army Form C. 2118.

Instructions regarding War Diaries and Intelligence Summaries are contained in F. S. Regs., Part II and the Staff Manual respectively. Title pages will be prepared in manuscript.

Place	Date	Hour	Summary of Events and Information	Remarks and references to Appendices
B.H.Q. BELOEIL BELGIUM	MAY 12th to 31st		Nil	

Forwarded C.R.A. 58 Div.

[signature] MAJOR
Commanding RFA (London) Brigade

www.ingramcontent.com/pod-product-compliance
Lightning Source LLC
Chambersburg PA
CBHW081459160426
43193CB00013B/2538